The Corgi Series

MIKE JENKINS
Laughter Tangled in Thorn

The Corgi Series Writing from Wales

Mike Jenkins

Laughter Tangled in Thorn
and other poems

Series editor
Meic Stephens
Professor of Welsh Writing in English
University of Glamorgan

Carreg Gwalch Cyf.

ISBN: 0-86381-703-3

Cover design: Sian Parri
Logo design: Dylan Williams

First published in 2002 by
Carreg Gwalch Cyf., 12 Iard yr Orsaf, Llanrwst,
Wales LL26 0EH
✆ 01492 642031   📠 01492 641502
✉ books@carreg-gwalch.co.uk
website: www.carreg-gwalch.co.uk

Supported by an 'Arts for All' Lottery grant
from the Arts Council of Wales

We wish to thank Seren for their co-operation in producing
this volume and for kind permission to include
material originally published by them.

To Marie,
with love

Contents

Mike Jenkins

Although born in Aberystwyth in 1953, Mike Jenkins has lived for many years in Merthyr Tydfil, where he was an English teacher at Pen-y-dre Comprehensive School. He has made Merthyr's radical history the subject of many of his poems and stories and has used the town's distinctive accent and idiom in much of his writing. Indeed, it is no exaggeration to say that the working-class culture he found in his adopted town has fired his creative imagination and provided him with an inexhaustible source of material. He takes his place with Glyn Jones, Leslie Norris and Harri Webb as a chronicler of Merthyr's past and observer of its rumbustious present.

A prolific poet, he has published ten books of poems, beginning with *The Common Land* in 1981, which includes poems about Northern Ireland (he is married to a Catholic from the Six Counties and is a staunch Republican, both Irish and Welsh) and about West Germany, where he taught for a while before settling in Merthyr. The town's bitter and often violent history became his dominant theme in *Empire of Smoke* (1983): making their first appearance here are the Crawshays, the local ironmasters, and Dic Penderyn, the worker hanged for his alleged part in the Merthyr Rising of 1831.

In his next collection, *Invisible Times* (1986), he

turned to contemporary Merthyr and the lives of its people, particularly the marginalised and underprivileged, and in *A Dissident Voice* (1990) he looked abroad to conflicts in Northern Ireland, South Africa, the Falklands and Northern Ireland; the 'dissident voice' of the latter title is that of Hilda Murrell, the anti-nuclear campaigner who died in mysterious circumstances. In *This House, My Ghetto* (1995) and *Graffiti Narratives* (1994), which contains stories as well as poems, we find him exploring issues of post-industrialization and social injustice as well as the potential of the local idiom. His close observation of the way his pupils express themselves brings to these dialect poems an authenticity and power that allow young people to speak in their own way. He can switch persona with consummate ease: one minute he's a skinhead, then a woman making crackers in a Merthyr factory, the next a pop-singer and then an alci down-and-out, all of whom are made to speak in raw and sometimes shocking language.

This successful attempt to give working-class people their own voice is seen at its most mature in *Red Landscapes* (1999) and *Coulda Bin Summin* (2001), and in *Wanting to Belong* (1997), a collection of short stories which won the Book of the Year Award in 1998. Among the many colourful characters who appear in these poems are Gwyn A. Williams, the Marxist historian and a Dowlais boy; a lad with a fetish for melons; a Duchess on a visit to a comprehensive school on the Gurnos estate; Siegfried Sassoon in Merthyr on VE Day; and a devil-worshipper on Valley Lines. Even more remarkable are the exploits of some of the young people whom the poet taught at Pen-y-dre. Several of the ten stories in *Wanting to Belong* are among the finest by Welsh writers in English that have been published in recent years. The writer has a keen eye for detail and a sensitive appreciation of what makes for poetry in what has hitherto been considered as 'unpromising' material for the purposes of literature.

Mike Jenkins writes in a unique style that is sometimes raucous and often sardonic, but it can also be tender and plaintive, with a deep understanding of 'ordinary' lives. His stripped narrative technique and vividly demotic language, together with the anger that bristles through his work like an electricity cable, make him a people's poet who is at his best in the many public readings and creative writing workshops in which he takes part. To hear him read his work brings an immediacy and depth that are not always apparent on the printed page.

From 1986 to 1991 Mike Jenkins was editor of the magazine *Poetry Wales*; a founder member of the Red Poets Society, he is still active in left-wing circles in the valleys of south-east Wales, particularly with the group known as Cymru Coch, the Welsh Socialists.

Chartist Meeting

Heolgerrig, 1842

The people came to listen
looking down valley as they tramped;
the iron track was a ladder
from a loft to the open sea –
salt filling the air like pollen.

Each wheel was held fast
as you would grip a coin;
yet everything went away from them.
The black kernel of the mountains
seemed endless, but still in their stomachs
a furnace-fire roared,
and their children's eyes hammered
and turned and hollowed out a cannon.

Steam was like a spiral of wool
threaded straight down the valley,
lost past a colliery.
The tramways held the slope
as though they were wood of a pen.
Wives and children were miniatures
of the hill, the coal ingrained
in enclosures on their skin.

They shook hands with the sky,
an old friend; there, at the field,
oak trees turned to crosses
their trunks bent with the weight
of cloud and wind, and harsh grass
from marshes that Morgan Williams,
the weaver, could raise into a pulpit.

A thousand listened, as way below them
Cyfarthfa Castle was set like a diamond
in a ring of green,
and the stalks of chimneys
bloomed continuous smoke and flame.

The Welsh that was spoken
chuckled with streams, plucked bare rock,
and men like Morgan Williams
saw in the burnt hands a harvest of votes.

I

I is the biggest word
in the English language –
some people yawn bored
as soon as you mention it.

I know people who erect crosses
made from it
and then refuse to carry them.

I know people who build extensions
onto it and call
those extensions their children.

I know people who would
like to keep changing it
every week like fashionable clothing.

I know people who hate it so much
it's become an obsession,
like a priest always ranting against sin.

In English, 'I' begins the sentence:
the other words queue up behind it
waiting for their instructions.

You must write 'I' with a capital letter
but 'we' with a small one.
Why? . . . well . . . as in God and Great Britain.

i know a person who tried to make it
mock itself, to disguise an ambition.
i know a person who thinks it will outlive
the exploring body, the inflated mind.

'He Loved Light, Freedom and Animals'

An inscription on the grave of one of the children who died in the Aberfan
disaster of October 21st, 1966.

No grave could contain him.
He will always be young
in the classroom
waving an answer
like a greeting.

Buried alive –
alive he is
by the river
skimming stones down
the path of the sun.

When the tumour on the hillside
burst and the black blood
of coal drowned him,
he ran forever
with his sheepdog leaping
for sticks, tumbling together
in windblown abandon.

I gulp back tears
because of a notion of manliness.
After the October rain
the slag-heap sagged
its greedy coalowner's belly.

He drew a picture of a wren,
his favourite bird for frailty
and determination. His eyes gleamed
as gorse-flowers do now
above the village.

His scream was stopped mid-flight.
Black and blemished
with the hill's sickness
he must have been,
like a child collier
dragged out of one of Bute's mines –
a limp statistic.

There he is, climbing a tree,
mimicking an ape, calling out names
at classmates. Laughs springing
down the slope. My wife hears them
her ears attuned as a ewe's in lambing,
and I try to foster the inscription,
away from its stubborn stone.

Laughter Tangled in Thorn

Dressed like a child
for our ritual Sunday afternoon
pilgrimage to the hillside:
your pear-shaped hood,
scarf wound like a snake
and red ski-boots dragged along
like grown-up things worn for a dare.

When I laugh, I don't mean it to hurt.
It is the brother of the laugh
at the end of our love-making –
rigid bones melting into blood.

The moor grass has turned
into a frosty yellow, its green
gone deep into hibernation.
We crunch mud, step streams,
in games which strip us of years
like the trees have been
of their leaves. The water
and your green eyes
share the only motion.

You see a red berry
and call it a ladybird.
I think of your city upbringing;
the seasons being passing strangers

through Belfast streets
where you cadged rides from the ice.

When the brook's chatter is snow-fed,
your laughter is tangled in thorn.
You discover an ice sculpture
mounted on a spine of reed,
and call it 'Teeth and Jaws'.
The light of your words
travels through it.

High above Merthyr, mountain lapping mountain.
You are amazed at the rarified sunlight!
When you speak, the numb streets
are startled. We leave the childhood
of the moorland, to grow taller
with a tiredness which is the sister
of when we lie, translucent and still,
on the single spine of our bed.

Discovering

Horizontal dancing
to the sound
of the spinning earth –
vulnerable as
              a frantic fly
yet ready to burst
from the house's pod.

With you, we discover
senses
        that logic's
data banks
had tried to process
into the pure expression.

Paper flaps like giant ferns
and there is a cave
in the corner of the room.
It is possible
              to pick up
shards of shadows
to make into tools.

And when your hunger-screams
fly in the primeval forest
they are
              half-lizard, half-bird.

Neighbours

Yesterday, the children made the street
into a stadium; their cat
a docile audience. As they cheered
a score it seemed there was a camera
in the sky to record their elation.

Men polished cars, like soldiers
getting ready for an inspection.
Women, of course, were banished
from daylight: the smells of roasts merging
like the car-wash channels joining.

Today, two horses trespass over boundaries
of content; barebacked, as if they'd just
thrown off the saddle of some film.
They hoof up lawns – brown patches like tea-stains.

A woman in an apron tries to sweep away
the stallion, his penis wagging back at her broom.
I swop smiles with an Indian woman, door to door.
These neighbours bring us out from our burrows –
the stampede of light watering our eyes.

Canine Graffiti

Some loopy boy wrote 'FUCK OFF'
in firm felt-tip on the white back
of a nippy-as-a-ferret Jack Russell.

Senior Staff spotted it while it shat
in the midst of a modern dance
formation – leotards snapped!

(When they weren't busy piercing ears
with sharp instructions, or spiking hair
with swift backhand cuffs,

they did have time to snoop on lessons
which exceeded the statutory decibel rate.)
They set off in pursuit of the errant dog,

skilfully hurdling its poop in the process.
They chased it into Mathematics
where it caused havoc by lifting a leg

45° towards the blackboard's right-angle.
Then through the Audio-Visual concepts room,
across the film of Henry V, making Olivier's horse

rear and throw the bewildered actor.
It hid behind a smoke-screen in the bogs,
sniffed out bunkers in the coal-bunker.

For hours it disappeared and Senior Staff
suspected a trendy English teacher
of using it as an aid to creative writing.

Finally it was duly discovered
by Lizzie Locust (Biology), necking
with a stuffed stoat in the store-cupboard.

Now you can see the distraught Headmistress
scrubbing form bell to bell in her office,
a small dog held down by burly, sweating prefects.

Orange-peel Man

Small man from up the Rhymni Valley
stunted to the size
of a mining gallery.
Silver hair the shine
of a butty-can.
Walks with a limp:
no compensation.

Every other Saturday's
relegation struggle, among
moaners and masochists,
behind the tallest pine-tree fans
he stands. Shouts
at the players like a trainer.

Might as well be in blind-black
at the seam, for all he can see:
yet he knows who has the ball
(invariably the opposition!)
and flings, disgusted, orange-peel
at players who ignore his tactics,
whose wages weigh the same as him.

Industrial Museum

For Adrian Mitchell

Hello and welcome to our industrial museum.

On your right there's a slag-heap reclaimed . . .
a hill . . . another slag-heap . . .
that one shaped as a landing-pad
for bird-like hang-gliders.

Notice the pit-wheels perfectly preserved
where you can buy mementoes
of the Big Strike and eat authentic cawl
at an austere soup-kitchen.

There mummified miners cough and spit
at the press of a button
and you can try their lungs on
to a tape-recording of Idris Davies' poems.

That rubble was a 19th century chapel,
that pile of bricks an industrial estate.
The terraced houses all adorned
in red, white and blue as if royalty were visiting.

See how quaint the wax models
of women are, as they bow in homage
to polished doorsteps, the stuffed sheep
at the roadside give off a genuine odour.

The graveyards have been covered over
and lounge-chairs provided for viewing
gravestones which tell of deaths from cholera
or pit explosions. I recommend their cafeterias.

In the ruins of the Town Hall the council
give public performances, meeting
to discuss the valley's future:
their hwyl is high and hiraeth higher.

Finally, let's visit the Foot Arms
(in memory of a long-gone leader)
and listen to the last Valley's character
who lives here, courtesy of the Welsh Office, in a
                                        tin bath.

Nant Gwrtheyrn

Perched on a grassy ledge,
like some rare sea-birds we feel;
learning the language of an endangered species.

And whatever the reasons that brought us,
the sea shelves at the edge
of our thoughts and the mountains
mouse our trivialities. Shaggy, purple head
of the lying yet waiting peninsula.

The wind's descant and harp-curves
of branches, together in penillion.
Candles are toadstools turned into a rage
of horses by Gwydion's flames.
I am dumb: my mind full of knelling
calls of quarrymen, pulled by the waves' ropes.

Wild goats tread the cliff-path
between reality and myth.
Shy and wary behind a twmp:
hear their night-time rock-fall
as they move in to graze
on pastures which pit beyond our step.

I watch the gradual renovation:
my learning tractored across rough ground
and voice beginning to fit the rhythm

of the carpenter as I feel
around and around, the eddying of Yr Iaith.

See, the granite lies in piles of nuggets
where no boat will beach.
High up to the mountain-top
the stone-supports hoist only cloud.

Listen how we talk and how the sea
rolls boulders from its tongue.

John

The sting of the fumes
and petrol had bloodshot his eyes
so they looked like an alcoholic's.

'Sir' was a word he'd abolished.
He only stooped to tend a car.
He saw bosses come and go
with fashions. In all weathers
he took his time.

His cap at a witty angle,
breaktimes we'd crouch together
secret sharers of the showroom.
Our ideas travelled further
than any of those pampered
cars could ever go.

His Valleys voice rising
to mountain-air elation –
falling to chatty river-flow.
He spoke of the Depression:
how he'd trudged on blistering feet
grey miles, a mirage of bread
becoming real ahead of him.

Some months after I'd left,
an old workmate, cool as coins,

told me of his fatal heart-attack.
A chosen son, I walked
at his own funeral pace
from the garage towards
a rusting distance I'd never attain.

Meeting Mrs Bernstein

Mrs Bernstein, the dogs sniff suspiciously
in your plotted neighbourhood,
while you open your door and your life
to strangers: trying to sell us your house
when we came for a piano;
sprightly body nudging a doddering mind.

You introduce us to your husband
who, impassively from the sideboard,
remains your dear boy.
With your father, the town's last rabbi,
your pride is framed.
In a small drawer
is tucked away your profession.

'Here they all are!' you say.
On a table's planet
the seas and cities defined
in pictures of your family.
Confident fathers and dark-skinned
daughters explained by qualifications.

Incongruous amongst a trilled dresser
and desk where you drum out the past
are Harvard and Yale pennants:
two sails beckoning your sight
beyond the whispering walls.

Mrs Bernstein, we listen to your playing:
Rachmaninov's chords bluster to America
where your anger declares itself;
during Chopin's night you commune
with your restless dead.

Down the garden steps you grip my hand
with a ring of bone. We cannot buy
this instrument of emotions
only your fingers know.

Survivor

They came from the arterial streets
of Dowlais, to the pill-box estate
wired to the hillside. Married
too young, for their bodies' sake.

You were, at first, a novelty
won at a fair. Then you cried
every night, dragging them from calm
of a deep sleep like a premature
birth again and again . . .
until he learnt to slumber and snore
nailed by bottles to his marriage-bed.
You grew up doing the opposite
of all the examples they set.

Now you smile survival at me,
like one of those old Dowlais buildings:
the Library propped by scaffolding
(friends hold you steady).
If I looked long enough
into the archives of your mind
perhaps I'd find the reason.

The time your father's bayonet-case
came down like a truncheon
onto your mother, you couldn't hide
behind their smoke or fan the fire

any longer. You hit his helmet-head,
so he struck out and you lay
like an imitation of the dead.

Tracey – the common name belies you.
You have reclaimed the black hills
of night with your boys on stolen bikes.
The sound of their engines
worries round and round your mother
as she sits and knits alone.
Your father's in a cot
crazily shaking its bars.

Dic Dywyll

I have banished God
further than the Antipodes
since my so-called accident.
He was the owner
of those mills of death,
his manager the old Cholera.
The preaching of Cheapjack remedies:
holding up heaven as a cure.

They took my eyes
and struck them
into cannon-balls.
My mask and its perpetual night
is known to the pit-ponies.

Crossing the Iron Bridge
I hear the river's voice
bring tune to my ballads,
the hooves of canal-horses
count beats and pauses come
as I breathe the welcome wind
from the west and eventual sea.

Night arrives and they all
share my mask: punchy drunkards,
rousing rebels and laughing ones
who sup to conquer daytime.

My daughter is the blackbird
giving flames to the begging hearth
of our basement with her song;
and I am the owl, I turn
to face their sufferings,
call them out to chase away
the chimneys' shadows. Masters
I magic to mice
under the death's-head moon.

Note: Dic Dywyll was a renowned balladeer in nineteenth century Merthyr, who was blinded working at the Crawshay ironworks. His daughter, Myfanwy, was immortalised in Joseph Parry's song.

Among Shoals of Stars

Each night the sea
tires of its slopping and slapping
and ascends the limestone staircase
of cactus-sharp stone.

It lies down
where sky has been,
waving away the blue
and only hooded clouds
show its occasional restlessness.

Bright fish with mouths
that globe, look down on me
and the breezy whish-whish
of sea-weed is the needled
branches of every pine.

I see the lights
of planes as they are out
trawling for dreams.
The moon spills milk
which I drink in,
before I too lie down
to sleep among shoals of stars.

Stallion

When the night's stallion
approaches us over the yellowing fields,
we see shafts of loneliness
in his eyes. The last wild flowers
have gone with the mares
he whinnied to, over the high-barred gate.

A barbed mockery of thorn-trees
and the two of us – jesting to catch
leaves feathering down – share
the hillside with the coal-hewn stallion.

Once, he had broken free, his spine
bridging the moor and the village,
hooves clicking the tongues of sleep.
Now, pushing flanks against staked branches,
he mules his raked flesh.

Invisible Times

Living in invisible times:
loneliness an economist's art.

Into the phone I take care:
testing the colour of each word
because of the spy whose wire
antennaes twitch, whose mouth
is a metal tube my voice falls down
to be shred like paper.

Outside, I wear a crustaceous coat,
knowing that the rain avenges
those gun-barrel chimneys
who wage war on the sky.
One day my scales will be eaten away
and flesh frazzled to cinders.

All around are the sick people
who cannot find the germs.
I tell them where to look:
under switches which grow on fingertips,
in clocks whose hands are trees
and pylons and flags.

Every day I'm on this journey:
looking for the computer who told
those lies, who caused my rejection.

'Facts are seeds grown hard
as bullets,' I would inform it.
But my search is aimless,
because the computer whirrs
in too many skulls to crack open.

The expert tells me I'm mad.
I see the motorway that workmen
are laying behind his grin:
it runs from the city of emotion
to the city of reason
and all purpose is within its rims.

Creature

Last night the sea heaved up a creature,
one I could not explain.

Half-boat, half-animal it seemed:
ribs of rusted tin, skull smooth as plastic.

My daughter played in its house of bones,
bouncing pebbles like syllables ringing.

She kept asking its name, how old was it?
Was it a dragon? Oil like blood dripped.

'I don't know!' I said (sounding unscientific):
she pulled out bolts of its neck to sit on.

I pursued it in books: the Bible dumb.
She ran in and out of its tunnel of questions.

Woman on Wheels

Don't look down on me!
I'm a remarkable invention:
half-vehicle and half-human!

Don't joke about such things?
Well, what is there left?
God's deserted me,
or I've ignored him . . .
whatever, it's neither blame nor salvation.

Don't look away or speak slowly,
I only grin stupidly
when I've taken too much gin.

Later, in the morning,
messages from my brain
jam in my throat.
My spine's a street
I can only walk in sleep
or in those photos once placed
in a case too high to reach.

Running on smoke not steam,
I become the mechanic
as I take my leg from the cupboard
to put on as you would make-up.
I prefer to numb myself

in poison-clouds of my making,
rather than face a sun
shining like instruments of operation.

You think I'm not like you?
It's true the world is full
of stairs and people climbing,
while I remain below
locked into pavement, gazing
as the building saunters away.
Yet I know some who are paralysed within,
so all they've achieved
becomes a throbbing, an ache
from a lost limb.

Our Living-room Parliament

Sitting in that cube of smoke:
your friend on a cushion of papers,
the women puffing in unison.
The fire spat out sparks,
while TV sportsmen
mimed to no ovations.

You and I on the edge of hard chairs,
balancing debate: our living-room
parliament. To finish a sentence
you'd to slice atmosphere with remarks.

Cream-cakes and tea, reminiscences and jokes;
but always the wrangles we relished.
I disagreed . . . I learnt from you:
nothing Headmasterly-wrought
about the way you listened
as I decreed worker and worker
outside traditions of culture and creed.

As the pills are no longer numbing,
I see how you were right.
As you're being eaten away
with the paltry food you can take,
I taste those Saturdays
brought back by wheaten bread.

One afternoon, all our talking stopped.
The house shook as though trying
to rid itself of troubles.
Miles across the city a warehouse of evidence
rose into the sky and was lost.
You'd seen the batons come down
on heads which favoured thought.
You'd seen the gas put masks
on eyes which would take borders
seaward from the common source.

At a road-block once, faced by police
with machine-guns to shrivel pride,
you replied in Gaelic. They glared
and muttered, thinking you a lunatic.

I cannot describe your illness
as *pain:* that would be as simple
as the formula I had applied
to your nation's present and past.

You stand. You'll stand as long as you can.
I'll finish my sentence for you to retort.

An Escape

On the mantelpiece, my mother's trophies
stand in line and wink at me.
They collect any sunlight
in our shabby room, where carpet stains
are bruises . . . his jealousy
those dents she couldn't dust away.

My Mam's at work again, on the tills
handling all that money which flows
through her like the facts
they funnel into me at school.
Keeping the bailiffs from biting
harder than any Big Freeze.

I wipe the condensation with my sleeve:
its smear like snot. I peer
through a film of dirt and damp
at dog-packs worrying the bins.
They search and tear for scraps,
their hunger sharpening canines.
Find more than in our kitchen!

It's the rain I despise . . . nagging me inside
with memories of screaming, fighting:
'Oh no! Dad!' . . . 'Get away you bastard son!'

But here comes Lisa with our dog
and her friends all wild in the wind;
and we're off to the little river,
to the tree-trunk bridge where our heads
will be leaf-light and reeling.

The Skin I Want

No more names:
no more 'Rem! Rem!'
'His dad's a wog!'
'His dad fucks little girls!'

       I will rise myself up.
       I'll dive into a sea-dream
       where I'll breathe like a fish.

No more poke and taunt,
point, cackle, croak:
ganging around me, with . . .
'Sly . . . sly . . . look at his curly black . . . '

       I will feel the rope
       a forgotten cord, meet
       the one guardian I can trust.

No more crying, no more fists
knotted in my throat and sweat
burning like ink when I work.
No more . . . 'Why can't you be like . . . ?'

       I will become someone else:
       make my branch of wire
       and my hill from a chair.

No more bulb bursting in my head,
glass piercing, painting the walls
with spatters of blood.

> I will turn out the light
> with a jerk of my neck.
> Make the darkness be
> the skin that I want.

A Newt in the Classroom

At first, I took it
for a plastic practical joke.

But she picked him up
and he walked, out of his aqua-sphere,
like a man on the moon.

I grasped the moment, as she had
the lizard: holding the idea by its tail.
We dissected him with words.
We passed him along rows
like a thought too icy to hold.

He was a clay god
each made in their image.
The sensitive Australian girl
railing against his imprisonment
in the grey box of her classroom.
The boy who tried to get inside
the skin so much he shrank
into a different dimension.
Too many calling him 'cute':
mistrusting their senses, even
their over-exhausted sight.

Under the sun of our attention
he was rapidly drying up:

'Get water from the Lab!'
'No, she'll cut him up!'

By Friday, he had died.
Turned white as blank paper,
while our walls were covered
with creations glued on
like his tail sticking to your palm.

Always the Ocean

For those of us born by the ocean
there will always be a listening,
an ear close to the ground
like an animal trailing.

I remember one night
I couldn't see anything of water
and I was sober as the stars,
yet below the tracked paving-stones
and gushing up through cracks . . .
benches tilted, clouds rocked.
I was a vessel, filled full of it.

This town at the valley's head
I've adopted or it's adopted me:
wakes fan from the simple phrases
and often laughter can erode
the most resistant expressions.
Despite this, I'm following the river
along our mutual courses:

to the boy on a storm-beach
hopping from boulder to boulder
trying to mimic a mountain-goat;
to the young man sitting in a ring
of perfumed smoke by the castle,
gazing at strings of dolphins
plucked by the sleight-fingered sea.

A Strange Recognition

Aberystwyth

A coincidence of eyes,
a lightning vision
across tables. Our notes
plodded, the out-of-date
statistics fixing us to seats.

Your long brown hair
I'd drawn in imagination
before we ever met.
My hungover head
too heavy to prop
juddered with the shock
of a strange recognition.

* * *

Outside the edge of the dance
I watched you ceilidh, swing
wildly with waves beneath your feet.

When we met I wanted to hide
in your accent, yet you mimicked me
as if learning a different language.

In the library your metal-rimmed glasses
framed your eyes downward, concentrated.
Away from shelved knowledge
we barely touched, I noticed
their green of sea in a certain light.

        * * *

Huddled and holding against the night-tide,
along the winding promenade,
stepping gradually into each other's histories.

The spurt and spume of breakers
hitting the sea-walls,
heat from our words making faces glow.

I rode the wind as I'd done
when a boy on the mountain:
then you caught me stumbling.

I lifted you up into air
which rolled and rounded our years
as beach-pebbles are eroded.

        * * *

The day after, I talked
of someone else the next summer,
teasing you with her name

and letters exhibited:
cruel reminders of impermanence.

You didn't tear with spite,
but clung on so tightly
I wanted to throw your hand
out across the bay,
knowing it would come back eventually.

                    * * *

In your flat exchanging tales
of relatives, like well-worn books:
you took me across the water
before I'd boarded a boat.

I collected your sayings
pressed by our lips:
making the bulbs shake,
floorboards creaking fears.

Our minds were ceiling-cameras:
a film director we both imagined
yelling 'Cut . . . cut . . . cut!'
just at the crucial instant.

                    * * *

It was a long way down
from the grassy hollow
above the cliff, a fit for our bodies,
to a station platform
and chat about domesticities.

From the seagulls' calls sharp
as rock pinnacles, to a park duck
alighting on a fence so near
I faced it lens to beak!

There was no ring of stalks
to be knotted round your finger,
only a timetable to make,
shunting our agreement into place.

But wherever we clutched
we'd glimpse the edge
and a rough path ahead,
always wary of falling.

Belfast

All around us the city was turning
into dust with dark approaching:
white dust from fires,
black dust flaking from buildings,
churned into the air
by a worry of helicopters.

Nothing else seemed substantial there:
I snuggled close to your softness
and the sheets whispered.

I shrank in your shoulder's cusp,
drinking your milky tones,
parched with oppressive dryness.

All you'd taught me couldn't explain
the guns' long hollows
and the one deadly mistake.

* * *

You spoke for me in daylight.
I blocked off my throat
like the streets we encountered.
Though firesides flared banter, argument.

I searched for the right expressions
but you kept the map
inside your head,
aware of the worst threats.

Times I thought you'd hidden
the voice I needed
and I'd act the interrogator
to make you confess.

Before sleep, it knocked at my heart
to be let in and I knew then
why you leapt at an everyday explosion
of noise from door or pan.

* * *

A mat of cheques
on the Presbytery floor.

If only your tears
had made the ink run
and blur, become a fog
of figures for a puzzled bishop.

They sentenced us there,
gave us 'Twelve months! No more!'
They tore up our documents
as if that's all we were.

Your family owned one brick
of the parish church.
In a place where names and colours
could be a crime, we decided to make
our own banners and search
for a renegade who'd accept
the heresy of a love condemned.

* * *

I believe it was that first
union of looks, or further back
to that part of our selves
where opposites had been built:
good and evil, right and wrong,
brick above true contact's soil.

Not a vow or signature
nor legal paper with single name,
not a ring of precious metal
nor a hired suit for the occasion,
not a black limousine one citizen
rightly met with a two-finger salute.

Careless of your earnest whiteness
I wanted to strip the veil.
I was actor and commentator
at the stage of the altar.
Priests and congregation embraced
at the renegade's bidding.

What I want to remember is speeding
towards the border, joke-sprung,
lost in Free Derry in our rickety car;
towards a wilderness of coast and bogland,
heading for horizons as they surely darkened.

Diver-Bird

People sat up from skin-baking or shade-seeking,
children on flabby lilos stopped squall-splashing:
not a pointy snorkeller, but a diver-bird.
'Duck!' someone called, as he dipped
and disappeared underwater, emerging
liquid minutes later as no human could.
'Guillemot' I said assured, chuckling.

Grey-black, shiny as wet seaweed
his head intent for rush of a shoal,
no periscope or radar could equal
that vision: beak needling fish
leading a feathery thread up and down.
I tried to swim out, follow him,
make clicking noises to draw his attention:
he ignored my performance.

Returning home, in reference books,
I realised 'guillemot' was just as absurd.
He was elusive here as he'd been
in the bay, no silhouette fitting.
Yet I knew he'd keep re-surfacing
further and further away, stitching
more firmly because I couldn't find a name.

The Memory Dance

(i.m. Philip Greagsby)

'Anything strange or startling?'
your catchphrase over the phone:
with few of the heavy steps
of your adopted home.

In an armchair, made higher by papers,
you sat under a blanket of print
snoozing with the radio on in case
something happened round the corner.

Your best friend, the ace reporter,
used to take you with him as scribe,
yet you never wrote us letters.
Now you're the only news that matters.

Leaving food to rot, the car's haphazard,
we drive off into the night
and encounter a frightened fox, dazzled:
his nocturnal sight we borrowed.

I cry as we descend the mountain,
the city so much less for your leaving.
I must meet you for the last time:
lying, not an ink-bruise to be seen.

Against tradition, we carry you, men and women
away from the path and over weedspread stones
away from communal plots whose names
you'd have tallied with a clerk's precision.

Ringing's no longer an ambulance siren.
Your elegant long-hand is waltzing
in your diary, to a gentler tone:
the memory dance has its own time.

Middle Age

Middle-age is when
you begin to get sensitive
about the crowd swearing at bald refs.

It's when your daughter's
History homework's on Dunkirk
and she asks 'Were you around then?'

You look in the mirror every morning
glad that you're short-sighted
and haven't got your glasses on.

Certain nouns slip out of memory
to be replaced by verbs
like 'to sleep' and 'to lie'.

It's when you want time
to go rapidly to the next holiday,
yet halt completely before you die.

It's when your appalling flatulence
is exposed to your spouse
and you don't even bother to say 'Pardon!'

You acquire irritable and incurable
ailments in corners of your body
and consider using herbal remedies.

You decide you need a new challenge:
working without a tie, your naked
adam's apple is swallowed by the boss's eyes.

Middle-age is when you take yourself for granted:
treat your dreams as pieces of furniture,
get rid of them on a skip.

It's when you're addicted to routine
and you won't admit it, keep on taking it
till you O.D. on those same old scenes.

Psychodahlia

Down in the darkest corridors of municipalia
is where the seed must've come from,
nurtured no doubt by a quirky computer
about the time of the Garden Festival.

It was to be Merthyr's own shrub:
a plant ideally suited to the area,
only needing to be oiled every ten years,
never losing its metallic beetroot colour.

'What should we call it?'
discussed the Parks committee:
'Mini triffid?' 'Spike drunkard?'
'ow about an ever 'ard?'

Without realising their irony,
because a stalwart councillor, after too many beers,
slipped on his way to a spaghetti
and skewered himself on the castiron cactus!

'DESTROY KILLER PLANTS!' screamed the local
                                              press,
but law and order merchants were impressed
by its vicious leaves and bought thousands
to surround the Civic Centre, schools and
                                    institutions.

Soon the forked flora had spread everywhere
threatening the soles of stray vandals,
so the Council named it 'Psychodahlia'
and the computer was made into mayor.

Gurnos Shops

An emaciated tree
clinging to its blackened leaves,
the wind snuffles chip-cartons.

The road's an aerial view
of dirt-dragging streams,
its scabs peeled off by tyres.

Clouds collect exhaust-fumes.
A man takes his beer-gut for a walk,
his wife follows on a lead unseen.

They won't climb up on plinths
where benches ought to be
and pose like shop-dummies.

Lamp-posts droop their nightly heads,
strays will do the watering.
Graffiti yells, but nobody's listening.

Yr Wyddfa Speaks Out!

It's summer again
and trip-trap trailing termites
carrying their backpacks
tread me down
sporting 'I've climbed Snowdon'
t-shirts: who's this 'Snowdon' anyway,
some kind of Lord?

It's rack and pinion all the way
the bumper to bumper
wanderlust like humping Nature
from grassy foothills
to flushes of heather;
get away from city-life
and breathe in fresh steam
laced with redhot cinders.

Oh! Not again! Here comes
the birdwatcher with two black eyes
jutting out, the silly old buzzard
hovering on an edge for hours
in his khaki plumage.

And there's nothing more boring
than a geomorphologist
labelling me with terms
like arrêtes and U-shaped valleys,

as the light changes
he's too busy turning pages.

Look at that snap of photographers
trying to suck the scenery
into those extended noses,
if I had the power to bring fog
swirling around my summit
to confound their art, I'd do it.

Those campers with butterfly nets,
at least they linger
to get moist with the dew
I perspire, try to listen
to my heart whose sounds
fall down to lakes, where my reflection
swims towards another winter.

The Talking Shop

In the Talking Shop
they spit out bones
which an auxiliary sweeps up:
they're crushed and made into gloss
for the latest glamorous brochure.

They talk white paint, plush curtains,
flowers and plants in the foyer:
they shred leaves of Chaucer
to garnish an exhibition.

Cogs of paper push hands
and a clock somewhere
justifies its existence.
They decide to decide later.

All the pounds left over
from multi-gym exertions
are heaped on the floor
for clients to sketch
in their frequent boredom.

In the Talking Shop
originality is a luxury
nobody can afford:
and if you complain
the word-detectives soon arrest
your mouth and use it to bin
the scraped paint, dead flowers, shoddy curtains.

Searching the Doll

Slowly pacing the beach
in age now not in sleep,
it's a cemetery
but I've come to dig.
Gulls wailing what's inside.

I'm alone again at night
in a waking trance
searching for that doll
I dropped, the blood-smirch
on its white wedding-dress.

My prints always lead back
to the cellar of that house.
A nine-month sentence stretched
to life on its camp-bed:
the memory condemned.

I chatted so readily then
hadn't learnt suspicion's martial art,
his affection the breath of air
and hands soft as powdery sand.
Soon became my jailer, my interrogator.

Buried me under his sweaty bulk
so my frenzied fingers tried
to take flight and reach up
to the single slit of light.
Dead birds washed up with the flotsam.

Vedran Smailovic

People dash across our TV screens
like sheep scatting from a moorland blaze,
they'll disappear over the edge of dreams
when we ascend to sleep away the day.

But, all of a sudden, within a frame,
a portrait animated and tightly-strung:
the cellist plays on streets where lame
buildings hobble before falling down.

His slashback hair is aging rocker style,
upturned moustache makes a sign of peace;
his two faces: a pizzicato smile
and mournful vibrato of so much grief.

His audience are the pavement wreaths,
from the distance come heckles of gunfire:
the amphitheatre where he once bowed
is a frozen skip of bricks and wires.

On a thin point he gradually spins
the web-fine veins of an Adagio,
while hearing the bombs' deadening dins
and fearing for that small bridge below.

The Ghost Boy

for John Davies

Until this I did not believe:
thinking it a figure of speech,
product of too many spirits
or, simply, the heart
catching up with the mind.
Though there'd been inklings
in strange places or
                              openings in dreams.

Here, he came as I lay
facing the ceiling,
                    vivid
without sunlight
                    he stood
at the end of the bed.

Mustard-flower hair in a sash
across his forehead
                         enquiring politely
what I wanted . . . 'Water?'
I shook myself awake
with a horse's snortling.
His one word kept repeating
'Water . . . Water . . . Water?'
Parched, but I didn't drink again.
Childishly switched a light on.

Once a farmhouse with doors
in all directions
                    once a café
for serious walkers
                    the boy
waited within original stone,
his spring tone
                    sipped by finches
observing me through a glass cage
where I sat munching.

Dŵr

Clouds –
whole valley-sides covered in berries
ripe and ready for the picking,
a steep rock-face with overgrown heather,
a flock of black sheep running
to be rounded up and sheared by the wind:
water with its roots in the sky.

Rain –
the drizzly seeds of droplets sown,
the slanting sea-strewn westerlies
which turn clothing to blotting paper,
the aching storms which gravel
into bones, making you shrink and cower.

Valleys –
scooped and scoured out by laws,
people cleared away like shanty-dwellers
bossed by bulldozers, memories
left to night-writers, to bells
tolled by feeding streams and rivers,
to drought and dereliction exposed.

Reservoirs –
acid funnels of the conifers
press down soil to stop it slipping;
to trippers they seem like mirrors,

but they balance water on scales
tapping mountains for its wealth.

Pipelines –
over the border, moving like a train
with trucks of coal, like iron and steel
liquid and molten, like the feet
of all those who had to leave
muttering 'Money, money . . . ' forced
against the gradient, longing for sea.

Chemicals –
a layer of aluminium the surface sheen,
the weight of lead its depths
and those substances meant to purify
unseen in a clear glass, lurking like radiation.

Houses –
the old person whose grasp of time
runs through knotted fingers and down the drain,
children whose minds become stagnant;
families knowing when it's cut off
water's precious as air when they choke
on the stench of their own cack,
as germs breed with cockroaches and rats.

Dŵr –
they've stolen the word, those safe-lock faces,
mispronounced it 'Door', reinforced and vaulted

below reservoirs where they've counted
profits from broken bones of village walls,
from a thirst which opens mouths
in fledgling questions to the clouds.

Mouthy

Sborin, sir!
We're always doin racism.
It's that or death, sir.
Yew're morbid, yew are,
or gotta thing about the blacks.

But sir mun! Carn we do summin intrestin
like Aids or watch a video o' *Neighbours?*
Mrs Williams Media upstairs ave got em.

Oh no! Not another poem!
They're always crap, rubbish
not enough action, don' rhyme.

Yer, sir, this one's got language in it!
It's all about sex!
Yew're bloody kinky yew are!
I'm gettin my Mam up yer.

Sir! We aven done work frages,
on'y chopsin in groups.
We ewsed t' do real English
when we woz younger,
exercises an fillin in gaps.

Sir mun! Don' keep askin me
wha we should do,
yew're the bloody teacher!

Once a Musical Nation

I'm tellin yew they're off theyr trolleys!
A whool famlee o' nutters!

I seen em through a gap
in ower Vesuvian blinds
with all theyr comin's an going's:
I'd rather them Rastafarasians
smokin . . . what-yew-call . . . grass 'n' leaves.

They play in the street
with all the kids (cept owers, o' course):
I think they're mentally efficient.
Course, I never let em ave theyr ball back,
just t' teach em a lesson.

They d' play piano loud ev'ry evenin
as ower baby's goin off, what timin.
They sing in Welsh an all:
I'm shewer they belong
to them Sons of Glenfiddich.

Why carn they ave a satellite saucer
like everyone else? There's effin 'n' blindin,
it's all in my diary, written down.
An even theyr anky-panky sounds
like a cage o' monkeys.

We're Merthyr born 'n' bred.
They come from bloody Aberdare!
They don' pay theyr poll tax
an let off fireworks in the New Year.

I'm tellin yew, we're goin off ower trolleys
now theyr eldest's learning violin.
We ave t' turn up ower telly . . .
an t' think, we woz once a musical nation.

Goin Fast

I gorra tell yew, sir mun,
carn keep it in no more:
now I seen er goin fast
like one of'em pooer Ethiopians.

See I know wha's up with er,
ow she've tried t' tell ev'rybody,
specially yew oo've bin ev'rywhere:
I think she fancies yew secretly.

It's er ol fella, see.
Aye, I know er famlee seem ordinree,
but I don' believe
in them words no more really.

Well . . . ee've ad er . . . y' know, sir . . .
reg'lar like ee wuz fishin,
she fells an ook inside er:
ev'ry pound she loses coz o 'im.

An I ave t' say, coz yew care . . .
wha cun we do? It's like on-a telly
an she've come outa the screen:
she's killin erself an I on'y stare.

Now I'm Sixteen

Well, I come in late
coz I wuz up-a Park
watchin the fight an coppers come
an I lost my watch runnin

an now I'm grounded

my Mam seen me smokin
by-a shops an I tol er
she smokes anyway
the silly ol cow

and now I'm grounded

we nicked a pram
an pushed it down-a sliproad
jus missed a Juggernaut
give my pissed brother a lift ome

an now I'm grounded

my Dad caught me snoggin
by-a bus-stop with this lush boy
oo woz over-age, ee says
yew'll get Aids, yew slag!

an now I'm grounded

me an 'is boy Darren
(they do call im Dazzy)
went to a party
an smoked wacky-backy

an now I'm grounded

I run away to stay
with my best friend Debbie,
but my parents come an grabbed me
sayin they'd kick me out nex birthday

an now I'm grounded

I swallowed forty magies
ad my guts pumped dry,
woke up in Prince Charles
to a diet o' runny jelly

an now I'm grounded

I smashed a bottle on theyr borin telly
an yelled if 'ey grounded me agen
I'd turn into a friggin Jumbo Jet!
an they called me rotten

an now I'm sixteen.

Merthyr People

for Steve Phillips, photographer

Waltzing Eyes

She's framed by the Zimmer, knits her arthritic fingers into each other, the crotchety texture of her pain.

The present is a tea-cup (no saucer), the stump of a candle, an egg-cup full of pins.

Further along the mantelpiece the dice are all on one, a photo of her grandchildren burnt white by her cataracts.

It becomes darker: her hubby's trophy, his leather-bound portraits a modest library.

Her skin is falling. At her feet are neatly-chopped logs. If she should rub her bones much harder, then a spark . . .

There's smoke from her grey hair. If only her flesh were grained like wood.

Behind her shoulders the plant has turned to soot.

You won't see her waltzing eyes till the flames begin.

Wolf Hour

It's wolf-hour in the precinct: pack of dogs, pack of boys. The mirror can't be seen. They reflect and swop features, triads with sharpened fangs.

Leaders face nose to snout, staring each other out.

Three concrete blocks where winners would stand to receive a battered coke-can cup.

The dogs are more patient: paw-leafed pavingstones are their horizons.

The boys have blurry feet. One jerks in incredible contortions, head taking off over the binned estate.

Hip-hop away, their leader's flung a can – 'Fuckin mangy strays! Don' shit yer!' His hair thick as an alsatian's coat.

It's wolf-hour in the precinct: the Shop Boys lurk in the background, from a ridge of reputation. Night comes, they'll snap up and pocket the silver moon.

Shadow Without Sun

Perched on a black and white pillar, call him 'Piggy', he doesn't care. His head's two stories above his sister.

His knee jabbers for him, saying: 'I'm loud 'n' dirty, I'm bloody mucky, open t' the air.'

Arms folded, captain of a team of one, holding the match ball, his cheeks blown up.

He's casting a shadow without the sun. She's in it, clutching her check skirt in case the wind . . . Her hair's the shine of a plastic bucket.

Her face conceals a window. His hair is curtained, tousled, already drawn.

Paper Escapes

Little black books
like school bibles
easy to hand
shiny as guns
telling how.to. punctuate.
if it's not written down
it doesn't exist
if in doubt
fill in a form:
marching columns
Roman legions
castle crenellations
a plan for life
no yellow-sprayed hair
no graffiti's sprawl
no rings in noses
no Pucker Georges:
polished as a scream
the set-off fire-alarm's
ear-splitting up yours
when catches break
opening like hand-cuffs
and paper blows
(tons of it)
with November leaves
becoming itself and screeing
down the banks, through

the sun-sluicing fence,
away across the estate
like the end of the year.

Moithered

She used it totally out of place
but natural as calling an infant 'Babes!'
The poet's moithered by all that pollution
like herself annoyed at my constant questions.

The word was *her*, chewing-gum twirler
giving so much lip and jip,
a desk-scribbler stirrer
using her tongue as a whip.

It was perfect for *flustered:*
I could imagine the artist
as all the complex phrases whirred
and churned, his hair in a twist.

No examiner could possibly weight it,
no educationalist glue and frame it:
it leapt out like her laughter
and my red mark was the real error.

Bethesda Brought Down

While the new road arcs
around measures waiting to be blown
and struts above roofs of terraces;
while the fountain's poshed
and the Korean factory's built
fast as the street's demolished.

Gone the potter's wheel where hands
made shapes which browned like loaves;
gone the dark room where prints
grew and bloomed with voices
meeting Parry's spirit in organ-pipes
of poem and song.

Bethesda brought down –
the civic vandals strike again,
each shattered stone a script torn,
only the Holm Oak protected by bars.
In the nearby office signers-on
are portraits framed by forms
and every season is angry now:
the east wind carries no applause.

Wee Maeve

She was eleven, freckly-faced and gingery-hair
sharp in class as the skrake of dawn,
chubbily confident amongst wild, wiry boys
who – knowing only mastery of the cane –
spent more time on the floor than sitting down.

I took quicker to the rounded vowels
of her Christian name, Maeve (an Irish queen)
than the baffling silents of the likes of Siobhán
and her surname, Connolly, had all
the ricochets of their history:
the executed martyr . . . how so much began.

One day she explained a rare absence
every word noted carefully, she taught us
more than I ever could, struggling for a say.
I imagined wee Maeve shocked awake,
her door battered down, the Para's invading
her home, dragging her Da away.

In that commonplace classroom in Clady
it was hard to see how she'd kicked out
and scrabbed such burly armed men,
must've brushed her aside like a pesty fly.
She described her revenge intricately:
mirror to the eyes of the helicopter pilot
targeting with her weapon, the sun.

The Pwll Massacre

We're playing high above the tundra zone
v. Pwll Boys' Club under 14's
on a pitch shared by sheep,
horse-riders, motorbike scramblers
and more dogs than Crufts.

We're in with a chance
till we count our team:
nine players including three keepers,
two of our star defenders
have discovered lager at 13
and there's no way to wake them.

Pwll are a small team
with the best (and only) oranges half-time.
They even have a tea-urn,
which is useful in the Arctic circle
somewhere north of Asda's.

We play a mystery formation
including at least seven strikers.
The pre-match team-talk involves
'It's a game of two halves,
but not equal players!'

It's their ref. and he's fair
as the weather. At 4-0 down

we're heading for their goal
only to be whistled for off-side . . .
our manager's warned for swearing,
their parents give him verbals
like snowballs packed with stones,
a collie brings light relief
with the most adept footwork
since Stanley Matthews . . .

At 12-0 down I give up counting:
the game's lost its point
because the local paper
only report the first ten!
We score a consolation
when the collie deftly noses in.
It's disallowed as he's underage
and anyway, hasn't signed the forms.

The ref. plays twenty minutes extra time
so his son can get a hat-trick.
Pwll parents are all gloating
like polar bears watching
a load of rabbits fishing.
'Ne' mind, son,' I say after,
'at sea level you'd have won!'

Three Observations of Geese

I

Geese are more powerful than horses.
When it comes to bread
they will spit worse
than any teacher or preacher,
the venom of their cobra-tongues
halting the young stallions
on the other side of the stream.
It's the noise of the whip,
of breaking in, which makes
strong animals bridle at the pair
of snaggling goose and gander.

II

Nobody can deny the pecking order.
Ferocious against each other,
beaks which snap shut
on wing-feathers, or jab
at eyes, the opponent's
shriek-honk of pain
sending them to the back
with the lame one and the other
whose call's still gosling-sharp.

III

Meticulous as cats they clean together
away from the web-waxy mud
on the tussocky moorland
they contort and pick
beaks now implements of relief,
till they sleep as one,
so quiet you could mistake them
for marbled boulders
left by an ancient ocean.

The Great Western

The Great Western laid to rest
in the dead centre, not far
from the barred precinct.
No puff left and the wheels
have long since rolled
down valley to Cardiff.

Above the bar, Sandie Shaw's feet
make whistles through tarry teeth
of regulars whose suits
are clinker and ash,
whose eyes refuse to light.

The big screen's bare
and hollow as a chimney,
the fag-machine has a hose
like a cooling pump.
On the sill's a packet of broccoli,
while BEEF's boldly chalked up.

Two spotlights are aimed
at a fan which is clogged
with dirt thick as coal-dust.
The window's a wire-webbed screen
into the High Street
where a couple of kids strut,
shut out in the dog-end dark.

The beer's strangely sweet
with a taste of sick or soap.
We tut at the evening's failures
ended here, with its ceiling
layered with years of smoke.

The Great Western in an engine graveyard,
as we three shovel and stoke
where tracks no longer remain
and the TV tunnel's beckoning back.

Snow Baby

You were a snow baby. We should've called you
Eira. You were almost marooned in hospital:
jaundiced face yellow as egg-yolk, clutched head
the shape of a shell.

You grew to your name, Bethan, grew round.
Your plum cheeks swelled to its sound.

And now in town you let the flakes settle in
your long hair, saying 'Ne' mind, I like 'em there.'

I played you *Ommadawn:* layers of cloud, frost,
hail and sun climbing till that lightning moment
when you were born.

Wrapped still through frozen nights, layers of a
nest taken from the strands of our house: broken
violin string, discarded lace and strap of a watch
you never wore.

Your dreams hatch and drift with feathers of the
pillow-bird you believe in no more.

A Heron Flies Overhead

In the scatterings of the year
the clothes will not take flight,
twigs and leaves do not stir
and the moor fades out of sight.

A tree-creeper scurries against gravity,
two jays are flowers of the air,
the geese snake water thirstily,
magpies are always asking 'Where?'

A heron flies overhead with calm
and rhythmic pulsing of the wings,
towards the west it charms
my senses with its rare passing.

It seems now like a prophecy:
what will happen when streams have gone?
Diggers will treat the mountain ruthlessly,
fumes and dust consume the songs.

Gwyn Alf

Never bin one f'r istree
lines o' dates
them kings an queens,
my memree no ware'ouse
f' such thin's, but ee . . .
ee spoke like one of us
took me back in them talks
I wandered to at first.
Ee brung it up t' date,
constructin a buildin
o' sights an smells
is stammer a-drillin
ands framin windows,
is fag the chimlee.
An oo owns 'is ouse?
ee seemed t' say.

Never bin one f' politics, mind,
them politicians on'y come
'lection time buyin ower votes,
I know enough t' know
a cross is thin as ink,
once 'ey get in
'ey'll all forget, but im . . .
ee wuz always from
round yer, no matter ow far
ee went, Russia or America,

ee laid a track
f' tram or train, is spinnin brain
'maginin a future town
where we'd get off, t' larf
an eat an sing under-a roof
of-a place we'd made.

Ee coughed is guts out . . .
death? never bin one t' say
tha much about it,
but when I yeard 'bout im
I couldn elp it,
my missis sayz, 'Don' talk soft!
Yew never even knew im!'
But I felt-a cement
drying my throat, my ead
poundin with-a wheels turnin.

Day A-Duchess Come

We ad a visit off-a Duchess o' Gloucester
(someone sayz she's arf German)
nobody's ever yeard of er before,
some cousin 20 times over
of-a bloody Queen.

The whool week the Eads wuz ravin,
never seen em in-a corridors
s' much time. Thin's woz done
what ad bin waitin f' years:
pot-oles on-drive filled in
jest before Tower miners appeared.

The Big Ead's muriel by-a stairs
ad its swastika scrubbed off
(las time it woz WANKER
right across is slapper).
Ev'ry little scuff woz touched up
an-a foyer woz like Kew Gardens.
A-deputy Miss Price woz up-a ladder
rubbin-a windows frantic.

She come by elicopter landin
on ower so-called tennis courts
(no markin's, no nets, no nothin).
More pigs 'an Cardiff v. Swansea.
There wuz a posh limo t' take er

up-a drive, red carpet an choir ready
an all-a swots sittin f' owers writin.

We woz stuck in-a room watchin
When Saturday Comes mega-brill swearin
an shaggin. Oo is she anyway,
what ave she ever done?
Presented er with-a miner's lamp 'ey did,
I'd-a give er worse 'an a gun.

People Yew Don' See

We're people yew don' see,
we're the invisible people,
ones yew turn out t' be
no matter ow careful.

We got clothes fit f'ra Jumble,
buy cans o' meat an cheap bread,
we obble off of the buses
weighed down by ower debt.

We're those yew don' want t' know,
bein old jest isn't the thing:
ow many newsreaders on telly,
ow many soap stars cun yew name?

Soon yew'll pack us away
to some nice shut-up Ome
called Daffodils or Sunny View:
on'y ower memrees free t' roam.

Wrinkles, grey air an shrinkin,
joints what do rust like a car,
we scrabble off-a paltry pension,
the pain-killers never go far.

We are the invisible ewmans
remindin ow close yew are
to the cemetrees an the Crem.,
t' the earth an also the fire.

Shop Boyz

Them boyz, them shop boyz
they'll skank yewr breath,
yew got any glass eyes
they'll ave em f' ball-bearin's,
they'll ave yewr gran's dentures
an make em inta lock-picks.
They'll ave yewr wigs
t' keep theyr Rottweilers
nice 'n' cosy at night,
yewr aunty's Woman's Own t' roll
out giant spliffs with.
If yew d'go by bike
make shewer yew chain it
t' yewr legs or else . . .
an if yew d' go by car
make shewer-a rust's so bard
it falls apart arfta 30 miles-p'r-ower.
Don' park yewr baby-buggy
f' more 'an 10 seconds
or yew'll find little Lisa
rollin with all-a coke cans.
They'll tax yewr boots
t' ewse as flower-pots,
yewr tooth-braces t' dust
theyr knuckles with.
Them boyz, them shop boyz
with baseball caps an baseball bats:

even-a pigs give up
when 'ey ram-raided Raji's
with-a ten ton truck.
They'd ave yewr flesh
t' skin up, if 'ey could find
knives 'at were sharp enough.

For further reading

Poetry
The Common Land (Poetry Wales Press, 1981)
Empire of Smoke (Poetry Wales, 1983)
Invisible Times (Poetry Wales Press, 1986)
A Dissident Voice (Seren, 1990)
This House, My Ghetto (Seren, 1995)
Red Landscapes, New and Selected Poems (Seren, 1999)
Coulda Bin Summin (Planet, 2001)

Poetry and Stories
Graffiti Narratives (Planet, 1994)

Stories
In Enemy Territory (Edge Press, 1981)
Wanting to Belong (Seren, 1997)

Anthology
The Valleys (ed. with John Davies, Seren, 1984)

For a critical discussion of Mike Jenkins's work see the interview conducted by Wayne Burrows in *The New Welsh Review* (9, vol.3, Summer 1990).

Images of Wales

The Corgi Series covers, no. 3
'Martyr to the cause' (right panel) by Michael Gustavius Payne; oil on canvas; 122 x 92 cm

Michael Gustavius Payne

Born 1969 in Merthyr Tydfil, Wales.

1991-1993	Glamorgan Centre of Art & Design Technology, Pontypridd.
1993-1996	Cheltenham & Gloucester College of Higher Education (First Class B.A. Honours).
1995	Athens School of Fine Art, Greece (Erasmus Exchange).

One Person Shows:

2002 *Brothers, Sisters & Dogs*, West Wales Arts Centre, Fishguard, Pembrokeshire.

2001 *Dreams, Fairy Tales, Myths & Nightmares*, Washington Gallery, Penarth.

2000 *A Modern Mythology*, Washington Gallery, Penarth, Vale of Glamorgan.

1997 Kilvert Gallery, Hay-on-Wye, Powys. Norwegian Church Arts Centre, Cardiff Bay.

Selected Group Shows:
2002 Contemporary Welsh Art, Beatrice Royal
        Gallery, Hants, England.
        West Wales Arts Centre, Fishguard.
2000 National Eisteddfod of Wales, Llanelli.
        West Wales Arts Centre, Fishguard.
        Kilvert Gallery, Hay-on-Wye.
        Washington Gallery, Penarth.

As in many of Michael's works, re-birth and destruction are played out against the darkening skies of rural or urban landscapes, with wailing trees, mute stones, or the too vivid blosoms of flowers. Vital to all these works are his painterly brushwork, the flickering marks giving an overall restless quality. Equally prussian blue and viridian pigments are worked into a chiaroscuro of light and dark with tremendous skill. Surreal though the paintings are, they have a compelling sense of rightness. They work.

Rosemary Holcroft for the West Wales Arts Centre

Contact M.G. Payne on: 01685 384533